THE FIREFIGHTER'S SON

By: Elizabeth Hall

Library of Congress Control Number : 2022917798
ISBN : 979-8-9870094-0-6

Website : www.thefirefightersson.com

To my husband Greg,
You will forever and always be my hero!

To our son Matthew,
Always chase after your dreams and make
each day your greatest adventure!

Daddy wakes up early
Getting ready without making a peep.

He puts on his uniform while Mommy and I sleep.

Before he leaves, he hugs me softly while I'm snuggled still in bed.

He kisses his Mrs., then carefully places his station's cap on his head.

For the next 24 hours, it's just Mommy and me.
We both miss Daddy, but we know how important his
job can be.

He goes on calls and puts out fires,
some with very big flames.

Each day is different; his work is never the same.

His work is helping others and doing what matters.

While Daddy is at work,
he drives the big trucks and climbs
the giant ladders.

In the kitchen, she puts on my favorite music,
so we can dance and wiggle.

We run errands, go for walks, draw,
paint, and giggle.

As the day goes on,
Mommy and I smile, laugh, and play.
Mommy is in charge, and when I miss Daddy,
she knows just what to say.

We are so proud of our hero,
and our community agrees.

When our neighbors stop to thank him,
he is happy and pleased.

When Daddy works on a holiday, our family always makes do.
We bring food to his station and celebrate with his crew.

When big moments happen, and Daddy
can't be there to see,

Mommy pulls out her phone
and sends him photos of me.

Every night, no matter what the day brings,
before we go to sleep, the phone always rings.

It's DADDY!!

When he calls, it's the highlight of our day.
We tell each other stories – there's always so
much to say!

We say "I love you", "goodnight", and
then hang up the phone.
Mommy gives me extra snuggles.
I know I am never alone.

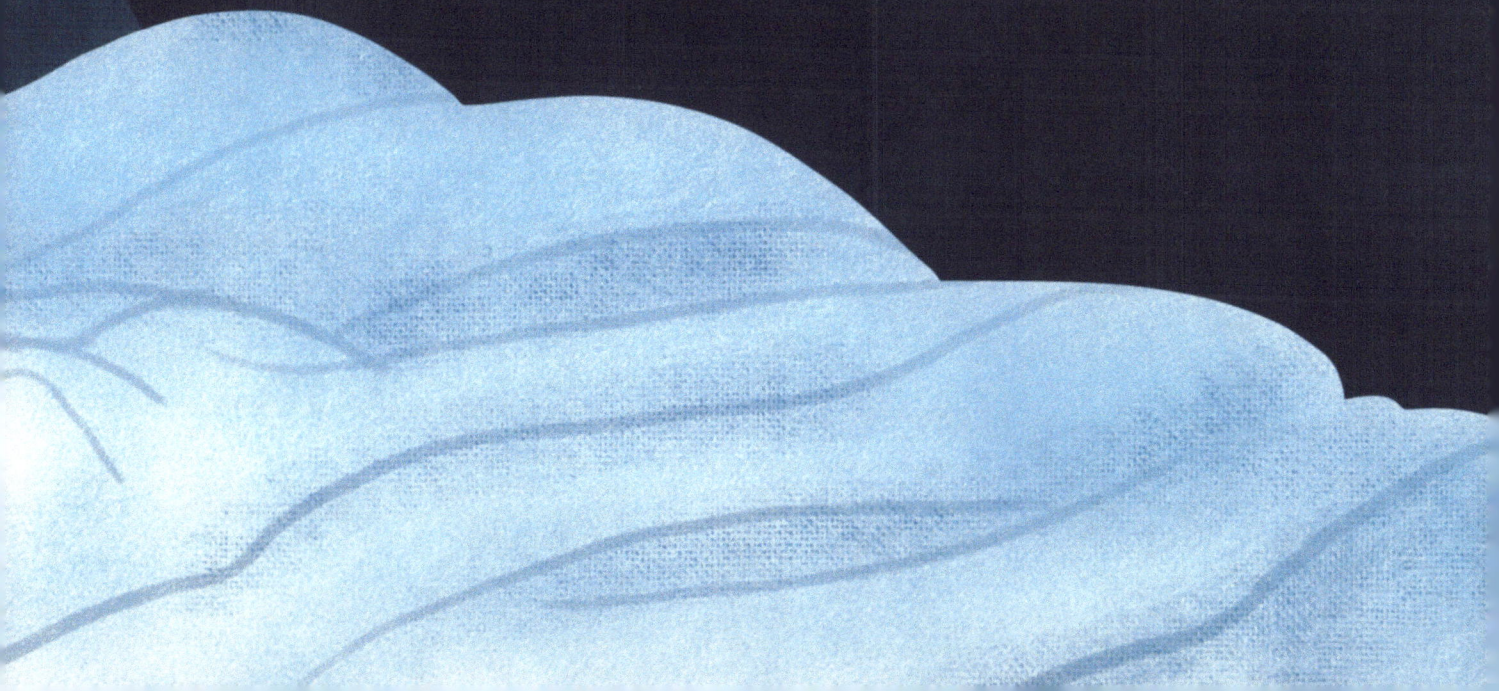

In the morning, we get up bright and early for a quick and easy clean.
We get a little messy when the house goes unseen.

We hear the door open, and I run for a hug
just as Daddy walks in.
He's finally home! We've patiently waited
to be together with him.

Mommy makes breakfast,
as Daddy tells us about his night.
Our family is together,
and now it's just right.

When our family is apart, we miss each other more.
When we are together, we understand how much
we are thankful for!

Photography credit: Angie Jean Photography

Thank you for reading this book;
we hope you liked our story. Please share a photo
on social media of you reading this book to someone you love
and use the hashtag #thefirefightersson
so we can see you and your family enjoying it together!

Lastly, thank you to all the first responders worldwide;
we are grateful for everything you do!

www.ingramcontent.com/pod-product-compliance
Lightning Source LLC
Chambersburg PA
CBHW060933150426

42812CB00060B/2640